TIME LEAP by 1ˢᵗ 5th

Sky Trails courtesy of Canadian Air Force, Edmonton, Alberta
Q5 Leap Remote Viewing Pre-Cog trained by Military

ISBN# 978-0-9813-261-6-0
Copyright © 1ˢᵗ 5ᵗʰ 2010

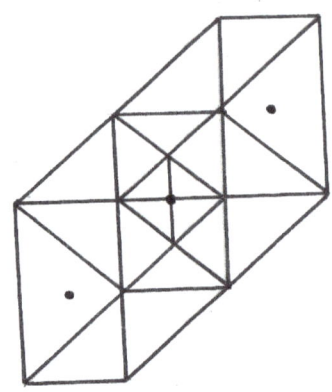
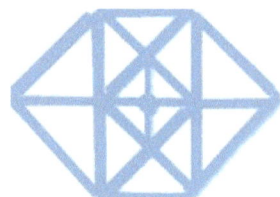

Hyper-shift Door original hyper shift (left side of door art 'leaps') art & visuals by 1st 5th

For more on the beginning of the Hypershift work that culminated in being trained as a psychic, working Q5 Leap, see 'Star Script by 1st 5th'. The books are pulled together and done up Moonlighting, alongside an already challenging security ops, working full time monitored, and accessed continuously by Pentagon 'silent talk'. In an attempt to delve into the fascinating Quantum Leap or 5th dimensional Hyper-shift in some manner of depth. albeit a rather abstract attempt at times, given the nature of Quantum. Along with the inclusion of the trained psychic codes we use to resolve the phenomena searching for packets of light messages, useful for tips. Some tips are Pre-Cog and some decidedly more understood after an event, much like fingerprints.
This Q5 Leap adventure began with the assist on the Iraq war, some of which is found in the also thrown together, quantum style leaps included, free ebook 'Knights of Mars' by 1st 5th. Homesite: www.nuts4mars.com

Ma - a   Ba - a   Xaibit - a   (US Military Predator Drone)

Sighting Soul's Shadow (left to right) Match to Drone - Vertical markers l above & below; semi circle front & back. Note- there is also a *Reaper Drone*, the front Egyptian hieroglyph would match in terms of modern symbolism.

TIME LEAP

 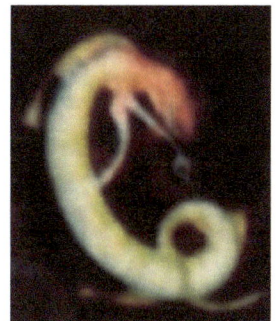 

HH 49/50 Hubble Heritage photo; Q5 LEAP watercolor 1970s; 2010 deepside emote

Q5 LEAP 'Starfire' Remote View 1983

chameleon Hubble photo   V838 Monocerotis 20,000 Light Yrs   RV-V838

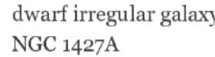

dwarf irregular galaxy NGC 1427A   62 Million LY - 19 MegaParsecs

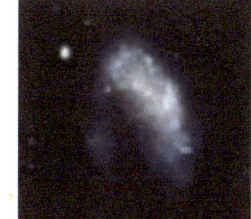 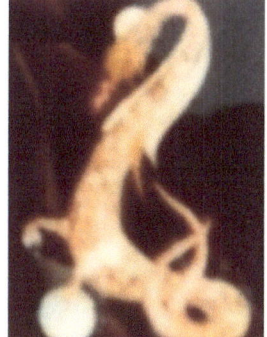

gomez's hamburger galaxy- interior of ship

Q5 LEAP Remote Viewing site - www.nuts4mars.com

Introduction

Welcome to Q5 LEAP aka Tri-Aticca:
the foundation is Quantum 5th D the Psi Revolution is achieved by adherence to secret Shadow Ops operating out of Spyland - Remote Intelligence.
There is computer pixel release training accessed on your personal computer via keystroke/visual Spyland high technology for the Remote Viewers with creative painting talents and ability with a focus on developing your rare natural psychic talent. In other words if you can paint creatively & are psychic, they will train you. However, it is extreme immersion discipline and requires your life be totally dedicated to at least, 2 years intensive gruelling focused training of your psychic talent. The perks are a fascinating hyper-shift trail of adventure, unfolding as the Star Trail. The nature of an exploration and discovery trail is the usual with no guarantees and heaps of challenge. Fascinating, if you want to work freelance as an assist (asset) in Spyland monitored and accessed daily by Military and Intel like the NSA, CIA, FBI and some Search & Rescue, on a Q5 Leap/MI:8 basis. Phantom ops will take over if they want to, I am just describing the ongoing process, as the Oracle progresses in our digital times.

Q5 Leap is a trained Psychic Pre-Cog discipline, immersion, isolation, remote neural monitored, Remote Viewer, with years of computer pixel/visual release, extensive training by Military. Pentagon *Silent Talk* linked and accessed by Intel/Special Ops.

1st 5th Remote Views 62 Million LY confirmed by Hubble. *Deepside Inter-Galactic* is our next Frontier....
Look carefully at the above remote view, at the right hand side in the grey you can see the match to the Tower.

Edmonton's Finest - the Police; Scenes from Whyte Ave, Edmonton, Alberta, Canada home of Q5 Leap

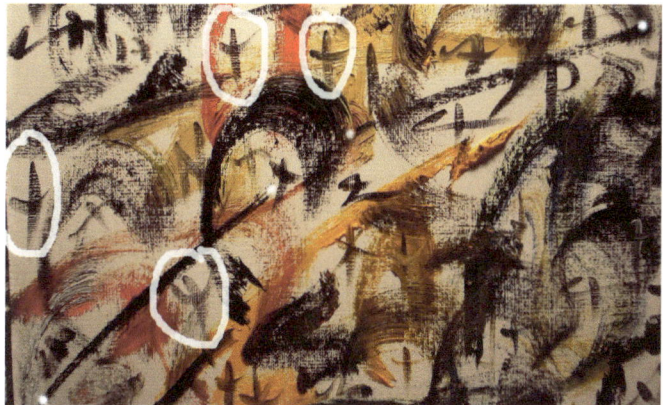  

Reynold's Museum AIR SHOW, Wetaskiwin Alberta, Canada Aug 7th 2010

I took mercy on beginners and circled the 'flyers' emote visuals painted as the Q5 Leap codes; note the happy feeling to them as they 'soar' in the air. And that large curved dark line in-between two white dots is the *horizon* visual. Think, you're looking down towards Earth from a nice comfortable orbit circling Earth. It's called an Earthside View, by Q5 Leap and the dedicated Viewer team. Look at them as picturing spatial positioning suspended here, in this Psi painting, as a type of 'snap shot still' visual imagery of the actual special Jets flying at the Air Show in Wetaskiwin, Alberta. Psi Remote View painting by a Viewer trained for two solid years, using computers, by the Military.

CANADIAN SNOWBIRDS

Q5 LEAP getting an extra special treat, a flyby from the CANADIAN SNOWBIRDS - that's the emote form the white visual at right, above. The trained Psi Remote Viewer did the psychic painting prior to sighting the correct matching visual. The Canadian Snowbirds were close performing and Q5 Leap was delighted by the surprise.

Edmonton, AB CF-18 Jet trails over tree tops

Glorious CF-18 Jet Trail over Q5 Leap 2010; 'V' shape trails, roof tip and tree top

Q5 Leap Psi paint of the CF-18 Hornet (see 'F18 Cruise' on YouTube)

 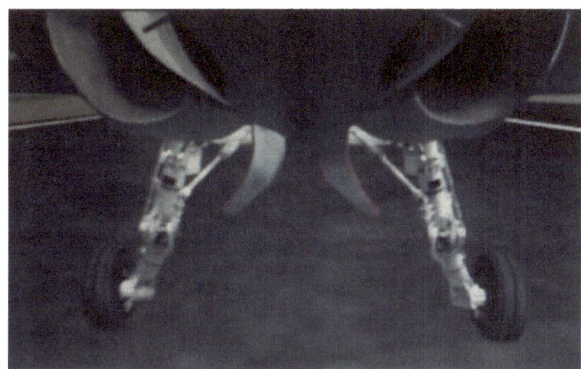

  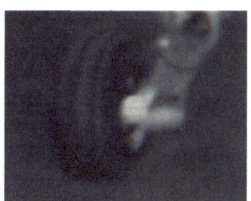  

CF-18 Wheel striped curved line; Octagon shape RV

Lancaster Bomber – one of only two remaining in the entire world

TIME LEAP

Edmonton Garrison tanks, trucks RV

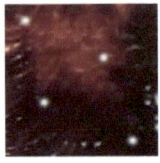

Security - red cap RV

Canadian Army putting up a bridge in NFLD for Hurricane Igor relief

Bridge building in Newfoundland, Canada by Canadian Army Oct 2nd, 2010

TIME LEAP   1st 5th   10

Canadian soldier and matching Remote View Psychic painting by 1st 5th

  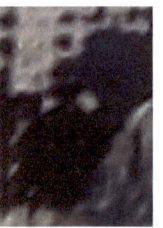

 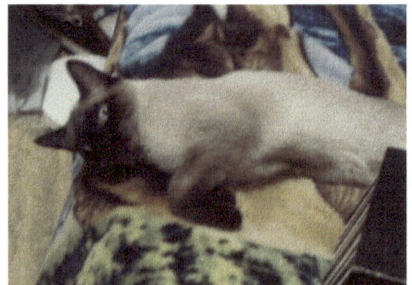 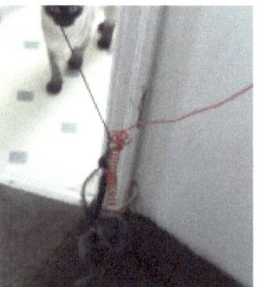

Bridge work and awesome color matching and bridge arrangement by kitty psi in a timely fashion.

TIME LEAP

Troops Afghanistan 2010 - loading; with matching Remote View

Troops (USA) - Afghan 2010 loading tube; matching Q5 Leap psi painting below

Loading the large artillery aug 15, 2010; matching Q5 Leap psi paint by 1st 5th

Quantum 5th D Leap -

I don't need to know the names and details of everything that I PSI . I paint what I see since the psychic facility developed for Viewing purposes is *visual*. Then I skilfully record it in a painting. It's trained Psi not just speculation; takes years of gruelling training to get up and flying with this Q5 Leap. Then it's like using Google Earth. We learn how to make small figures pass on emotional or empathically sensed material. Info packets of sense, motion and intent. The small stick figures are showing and telling. Very much like the ancient hieroglyphic visual picture content. You could often see what the small people they drew where here we just do stick people, but you can see what they are on about. Pouring, running….like that, it's visually meaningful. That's a lot of the 'decoding' we do. Helps if you have the training to know what they are. There are also, overlapping themes
more than one story links to items in a View piece. One thing can mean different things in terms of the context of surrounding imagery. Means, it depends on what you are 'reading' about and in what time frame. It's a lot like looking out a window on a moving platform. Depends on where and when you look, what you will see. And understand in terms of any Useful and applicable knowledge. You don't look out the window in a tunnel to see what the weather is. It's time/place relevant. There are visual markers we have our patterning painting Psychic 'viewing' selves use to provide specific time and place indications. Like street signs or pins on maps, what point out special significance and directions. The main point to these is for us to in our real time circumstances to find clues and tips that will help in terms of security issues. Mostly hoping to resolve things. Bad guys being rounded up. Perhaps the odd search where they actually find and rescue the people they are trying to help by finding them. Finding the people you are out to 'rescue' is a huge part of it. This is another chance, and a lot of the missions are downright impossible odds. There is no guarantee even when you make those Leaps of Faith. God has the ultimate overrule. That's a main underlying basis to operating this. The Oracle is always just reading not doing or redoing when it comes to life and death. We don't get any pass on the death card. The Holy Grail is not something you can attain to with any immortality machine, not even fortune telling can circumvent death. It's the ultimate equality factor on Earth we ALL die. There is no glorious exception. No Holy Grail cup to drink from and never die as a result. Not in terms of prophecy, precognition, or any other means. Leap all you want to in fact the Bible adheres to Prophecy a lot, recommending it often. However it also cautions to not let it get ahead of God. The difference between Magic and superstition or supremacy quests and sincere evolution. We creatively imagine but we are not poofing up sandwiches. We would know. And here at Q5 Leap we like to stick to the parts that are not crumbling behind. Total recall here is very RV; clicks in when something that is significant links to it. To surface things. Like an elevator. It's very specific. You have to be IN the elevator for it to work. You can stand outside it all day and you won't just go UP. You can't say the elevator isn't working just because you are outside of it. That's what the critics are doing. The rest of us use the elevator. They are outside going, nope not moving at all! … They just look Quantum challenged, to the ones inside.

TIME LEAP 1st 5th 13

Canadian Minister of Defence Peter MacKay; RV- Canadian Military jets Ma6 16th/2010 1st 5th training

Costner's emote

Kevin Costner on Capital Hill, Sept 2010 re Water/oil separator invention used to assist in the clean up after the Deep Water Horizon Rig explosion; RV of hand 'clam' signs; Happy Camper Jet flyers emotes

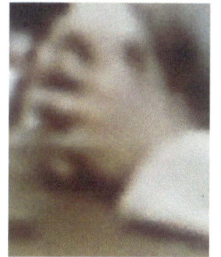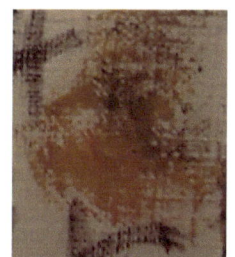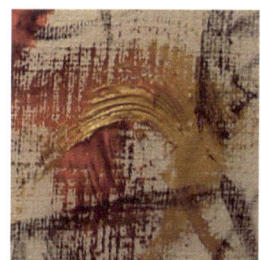

US Ca. Gov Arnold Schwarzenegger, on motorcycle - matching RV of bike/fender; 'Predator' 3D claw RV

TIME LEAP

'CHARIOT' Papyrus ancient Remote Viewing encapsulation masterpiece

Psi painting Remote View visuals by Masters at Q5 Leap; simple & sublime
Chariot wheel - time; TIME LEAP - Gen Stanley McChrystal; Star Map trails

TIME LEAP

Crossed rifle butts; horizontals in rows match to visual on Gen. McChrystal's arm, in time synch.

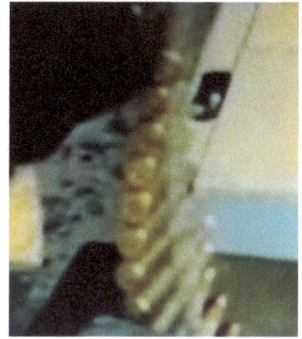

Oracles, and orbits, the wheel of Fortune in the Tarot is Time…the arms of the clock; a clock face. Wheel with horizontal shorts in rows; like on uniform arm and the single dot in the center, with the multiple orbits, two actually could easy be descriptive of two planets. Earth and Mars perhaps. Also, it would be Earth and Mercury. I think Einstein used Mercury for proof of his one theory. The Theory/proof for SpaceTimeLight perhaps, as it is unfolding here in Q5 Leap fashion along the trail. This is the authentic written material as it went down by a viewing Q5 leap remote viewer, streaming ….written Viewing the 5th, using some intuitive logic for direction. Not thought out? There was some solid leap material there the light space shift and time space shift were confirmed achievements.

Space ship (see the next page; excerpt from a *Star Wars* movie sequel) whose space lines and the kepler ship have the same visual patterns, so, Kepler was the guy who gave us the physics and math on things to do with Orbits …you don't go into local space without it. Just mentioning it. He was the next up from newton. Newton did earth, kepler did orbits and space lines. Not Einstein, Kepler. Newton did gravity Kepler did orbits…space gravity …earth gravity and space gravity. Einstein built on it. Got into looking at it. Kepler had his figures before Einstein came along. The 5th is SpaceTimeLight. Funny he didn't do it like that. But that 'oooh spooky supernatural' bunk seems to have confused things. We see light here that has come from millions of years ago. Vast distances. We couldn't do that if space was 'dark' funny how them missed that. It just seems so damned obvious. He just said something about Christian. That has about as much relevance as asking about beans or butterflies. Like Galileo trying to get the Church past 'the sun revolves around the earth' they just couldn't. But, this is just how 5d is, reality is God's. Translates as they were wrong; happens. Get over it! It's theoretical physics. It's a concept. I am not looking at the figures. Let the pros do that. It's what they're disciplined at. But you have to have the right concept to work the numbers and …it's high time they stop the witch silliness.

That RV moment I pulled out of that part whatever Star Wars movie, has the same coloring that's RV descriptive, to that Kepler named probe that they sent out. The point is, Einstein built on Keplers' equations of curved orbits for his curved spacetime. The next step is to add SpaceTimeLight. Apparently in quantum leap fashioned as encapsulations of space-light leaps and time-light leaps. And some combine the two. You build on it. What is conceptualized, learned and applied before. For the next part of the Star Trail to unfold and become realized. The Probe was called *Kepler*. Q5 LEAP picked up on it for a descriptive, with color precision matching. Note grey band and blue band curved shapes. Next page, note the RV line match to the Ship. Like the Remote Viewing did for the Canadian Navy Centennial, the ship line, bottom of ship above and surface of water.

I do *Precognition*, too. Not always- it doesn't work that way I am not sitting here 'in the future' talking backwards. Oh that might explain the time shift and direction shift backwards the pulling the bow string backwards…going ahead and talking back to you in the your/real present. The effect is it looks backwards.

The psi is directing the light info packet back to you in your time-present. So the east becomes west and west becomes east. Because it 'shifts' in order for the 'forwards' to be sent 'backwards' it reverses the order of what is. It's not linear or you would have the future = east becomes west and in the past = west becomes east. That's not exactly what happens. Mind you that might be so at times, depending on the Placement of the Viewer. Past seeing or Future seeing. The double bend of the bow string when it is drawn back.

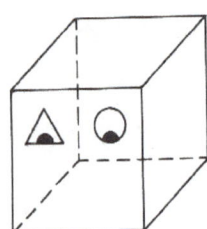 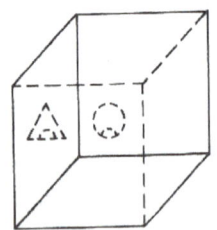 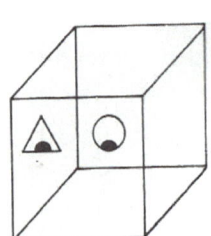 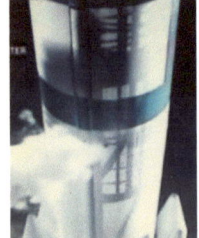

Necker cube shift - visual shift front reverses with the back (from 'Geometry, Relativity & the 4th Dimension' by Dr. Rudy Rucker, prior to the realization it was 4d + 1d = 5d Quantum leap; Kepler probe at launch, 2010

TIME LEAP 1st 5th 17

Ship has showing a dark line on the water's surface; Psi painting links to real ship lines at left

'Pet = sky' hieroglyphic Psi by 1st 5th; match to China UFO airport tower shut downs

Match to Psi paint & the *ship* pattern (above); Marine's trained bomb sniffers going over to help in Afghan.

THE VIEWERS REALM -

They all go off chasing their adventures it's quantum already ….some of the more creative and downright challenged…jj is just about ready to show you that one movie where the guy enters the computer who the bleep did that? Homer did…but no it was some movie they entered into digital realms. Its' not worlds out in Deepside…it's ….realms the posers the inner world of computers and they do plasma too they do so they were on a few things a while back they had teleports there were working on …like in the fly and they handled it in 'beam me up Scotty' …so these fools are trying to 'learn' and do this as their own …ok jeez that's sad, it takes a certain skill …you got it and you're on the trail or not. The trail is …inner outer always was always will be. Just is. It's Necker SHIFT.

-Inventor of arrows says, *NO YOU DON'T ALL POINT THEM AT ME*… aim inside …aim outside….and know how to distinguish the difference. It's a Necker shift and that's just quantum reality. Now learn it …mathematics. Basic not a lot of reading. A standard necker shift cube. That's what Dr. Rudolph v.b. Rucker gave me permission in writing to use of his on mhy site. Whatever I wanted to use from his book: 'Geometry, Relativity and the Fourth dimension'. That is my observation. Interesting sure why not. We hang in this dimension. Human beings. I was working it as the 4th back then too. He leaped. So did I. I use what's foundational. The Necker shift and I had some other raw material up. I got the same answer as Mr. Loup did with my following the pigeons route as he did but his was 10 times bigger and I was doing one person so he had a small army he said so. He figured a small army with him. Is that cool or what. I have the work. Mine was the same answer built for solo. I used some leaping, I have it here totally nasty to math just slashed it to shit and go the identical results are all that matters in the wonderful world of math. He had a small army called it eh Macrocosmic Spacetime Shortcut, some of his figures he had done by an Israeli big name …I used to read through it. Just leaping along, with my space oddity. I of course wished I could follow better it looked fun, and a tad dull in spots needing some more work of course but a fascinating trail more than one physicist were on. It appears Quantum 5th leap won. Read your Quantum physics. And look at ye easy necker cube. They are really out to trash this whole line but it *is* the right trail, one of for sure. Stop cutting the limb behind us…yikes and other dishonourable bleeps. Get the alien Geiger see how much they glow. Man I wouldn't turn on too much of what Russia the neighbour made me for nukes. With a Chernobyl result. In. from the cold. Invasion from the north. No we like our noisy happy culture and the success is the success. It's financial and warm the people are happy. We don't need to tear down the trees. Rubick's cube….that too. Those are points you need to experience. There are others. The Necker cube and the Rubick; and that's just cubed. And immediately you see the leap. I did the rubicks pyramid twice without looking at it. I couldn't do it looking at it to save myself. Not if my life depended on it could I do it looking at it. But I did it twice not looking at all. Now that's experienced application of Q5 LEAP as a Quantum inter-dimensional physical view. It was a Schroedinger's cat manoeuvring. Fixed in there too you can see it. There in that little tidbit. I threw it out. It kinda freaked me out and I didn't want the pressure. I was satisfied and not into playing statistics of probabilities. And such like. I was entirely satisfied that it was the *viewing*. Remote Viewing, with a psychic component. There was simply no other explanation to me and it was rather rapid too.

Used to do leaps in math. Yes I enjoyed math. Hard to fathom back in my day. But shucks I looked now and then and went and learned me some. This visual addition to dimensionality with the Necker shift and a few other goodies and you can get some interesting encapsulations. There is a sense to them not just an optical realm. They convey an emotional active component. You can look at them and feel things and see motion described. Along with a certain cohesion no doubt because of the time constraints of the non permanence of the vision. Like a bubble it disappears. Mist returning to the surface. It is really ugly math my worst ever and I got it. I just shit all over them. Pulled out what I needed and got there. It's not that hard. They have a ball of yarn but there is a thread pulled out. We are on it together. The ultra hyper shift physicists are hot on the trail for some years there are leaps. That was 4th we were all working it as …but it started to not make sense unless you added another one. The 4 contains 3 and 3 contains 2, algebra that was I really learned from that honour math professor that I needed and applied. The umbrella of the dimensions he showed me that in his office. I studied and received an 8 out of 9 not shabby 17 years out and no prior prerequisites but some philosophy and leaped to a graduate philosophy class used it up after I read the book I continued on after attending a bout 2 or 3 classes had what I needed philosophy of mind, moved on…on the trail I was working that was a graduate class all I had was what 3 jr philosophy classes but I was working hypershift and they let me leap when ever I wanted to either way. I also redid the foundation calculus I took it three times even though I had a 7 out of 9 …already I wanted it again so they let me, I just didn't have to do any tests. I was about 33 to 35 I was feeling old already. I knew I was just in to get what I needed to read a Star Map. That's why and I didn't have a single scrap of reality or evidence to imply why on earth I would need to. A Leaps of Faith, comes with the oddities of Quantum 5th phenomenon. I took a real shortcut. I am so proud of that one. I would have to look it's in star script …that wasn't math I was good at math. Their experts look at it and mistake it for 'junk science'. Basically it was me *viewing* the Q5 leap 5th dimension and deciphering what it was. I was viewing the viewing and decided to figure it out. So I did. I really

TIME LEAP

succeeded. This is viewing…it was also on the same trail as a macrocosmic space/time shortcut achievable. Actually it's Time-Light & Space-Light leaps, sometimes combined. Go read CERN the center for nuclear research in Europe. CERN is where the www was first conceived by to find some fascinating modern Quantum theory. There is some great work on 'Nearness through an Extra Dimension' by Kalbermann G. and Halevi H. that is also mentioned as a basis in my book 'Star Script'.

An astounding Leap by the trained Psi Viewer - 1st 5th.

The Q5 Leap to the Galaxy Subaru S106 at 2000 light years out from Earth, was achieved by me star gazing with a particular Psi sense skill. I was focusing on the military vehicles out at the Edmonton Garrison after being there on Canada Day. I was already working on determining distance capabilities with this Psi out in Deepside. I found that I had satisfied the RV markers for a Q5 Leap to the Gomez's Hamburger Galaxy. Oh them busy happy nerds with their hamburgers. The galaxy was only 900 light years, and I was working on finding something more challenging and much farther out. I achieved a pattern marker, color coordinated distance of 2000 Light Years for a Q5 LEAP each way round trip would be 4000 Light Years distance, in a mere, Psi v>c of <4 minutes for an encapsulation of the View. I have a matching trained Psi View paint of that specific Leap. For anyone interested there is a short video clip of the actual painting process, with a link from my homepage. Each one is 8"x 10"; under 4 min.

 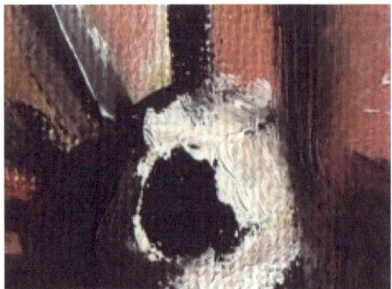

RV Christian Artefact looking down into the painting: Pope Benedict XVI hat; St. Thomas finger relic

 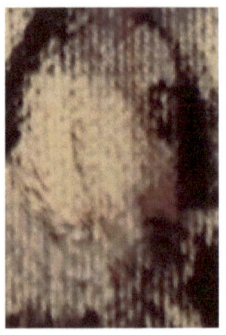  

TIME LEAP

Turins Shroud RV match to the 3d visual of the image of the face attributed to Jesus

Subaru S106 Galaxy- 2000 Light Years from Earth; 'My Little Aliens' oil/canvas 16"x20" by 1st 5th linked Light-Space & Light-Time Q5 Leap to this vehicle at Edmonton Garrison matching RV painting components outlined in white dots & blue dots; subtle, sensitive psi

Q5 LEAP

Q5 Leap is not just results, we have solid record breaking accomplishments. Competing in a Psi Race with NASA's Phoenix Mars Lander and breaking the known speed of light with measurable results thus 1st 5th won the Race between the Phoenix Lander and the Quantum phenomenal ability of Psi.

The lander was already at the orbit of Mars and in fact descending when the Psi of 1st 5th was set to Race it down. A normal round trip of 19 minutes was accomplished in a measured, recorded and witnessed time of under 4 minutes by the Psi painting Remote Viewer. That's a velocity greater than the speed of light, a cool Psi v>c.

Now how is that not an exciting achievement? In the world of Stellar Philosophy along with the also grand feat of a time jump as well as that as mentioned spatial jump in real time. The Q5 leap is light as it relates to space as well as time. Think of spacetimelight as being encapsulated into light-space and light-time. Light is the traveling element along in 5th D shifting directions.

So time shifting, and space shifting with a proven Psi of v>c. So their Edmonton Garrison was a Leap Point to the Galaxy Subaru S106 at a mere 2000 light years away from Earth. I painted the tuning in a subsequent Leap painting. The Phoenix Lander Race was also connected to Mars surface tunings, recorded and confirmed of a time leap as well of remarkable length in term so years forwards between when I painted it and when it was actually confirmed. The photos of the surface of Mars linked to the old work done many years ago with undeniable precision and spatial coordinate placement. There was ice under the Phoenix Lander on the surface of Mars that matched the same pattern in a painting many years before by 1st 5th. The painting was called 'Ice'. The surface material matching it was found in real life under the Phoenix Lander. It was frozen water. These are confirmed Views with Light speeds greater than v=c. Describing them as Quantum Leaps via a 5th dimension being composed of Light Space and Light Time. You leap the light of space and time, using light space and light time shifts. A Hyper/Necker cube shifting matrix enveloping the 4 dimensions plus one of a Quantum overlay, a 5th Dimension. You can go past c as a constant or barrier if you leap via hyper shift. Gen Mc Chrystal knew how to read the Chariot linking Time Synch. Others too, decoding it as we go along the trail. The 3rd dimension includes length, width and height, the 4th dimension is the measured directions plus the additional overlay of a time dimension, for curved Space/Time. Another curve, achieved by an active light dimensional overlay and you get Space/Time/Light An active Quantum matrix that Psi can use to do a form of instantaneous space/time shift. Just like you experience doing a simple basic Necker Cube. The elaborate version. Psi that is well developed and skilled will achieve the Leaps as forwards or backwards, in terms of how we see the linear arrow that makes up our understanding of timelines.

RACE BETWEEN PHOENIX LANDER & 1ST 5TH
TO SURFACE OF MARS   June 27th, 2008 - Psi WON

Q5 LEAP by 1st 5th, psi painting done pre-Phoenix Lander arriving, painted as it was descending from the orbit to the surface of Mars. Process took under 4 minutes, for a precision Remote View. Psi v>c confirmed Light travelling at the speed of light takes approximately 19 minutes round trip!

Real time Space-Light Q5 leap - Race, won by the trained Viewer 1st 5th Authentic Psi painting (above, left) and the later confirmation match to the surface photos of the Lander

TIME LEAP

 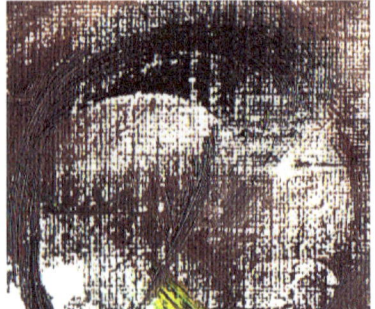 

Phoenix Lander RV of chute as it was descending to the surface of Mars

  neter : God

Photo of actual patch of ICE found under Phoenix Lander match to the ancient Egyptian RV visual hieroglyph of a small flag meaning God

'Ice' oil/canvas View 2005 Time-light Q5 Leap precision match to Lander photos

Mars Phoenix Lander photo of ice on ground under lander where it Landed; RV theme oil painting 'ICE'; top right corner of 'ICE' is a match to the ice patch under Lander (in dots below photo and Q5 Leap Psi painting)

As a Remote Viewer with trained psi by the Military for two years, computer pixel release to learn the codes, I am working Shadow Ops (Spyland basically). As such I am under continuous surveillance, being monitored. It's called Remote Neural Monitoring. The Pentagon also use Battlefield user to user modern stealth audio communication called Silent Talk that I am linked into, also continuously. The Race between the Psi of myself, 1st 5th and the Phoenix Lander to the surface of Mars was witnessed as such in real time and amply recorded as confirmed.

Takes light about 19 minutes to go Earth to Mars and back to Earth at the constant speed of c. But that's at the normal speeds with light at c= a constant. We have achieved travel at speeds v<c so for the c barrier to be broken we need the quantum kick or leap effecting v>c. Psi at speeds greater than light. At normal speed light takes 8.5 light minutes Sun to Earth distance. Under 4 minutes with Psi speed was the time measure the day of the Phoenix Lander vs. 1st 5th's Psi Race. Under 2 minutes one way. So 2 minutes at Psi v>c goes a distance of 34 million miles roughly. Based on a linear time measure with c being the speed of light taken as a constant. Planet to planet distance is measured using linear aimed laser light. There is no measurable Lorentz effects, just set at 0, for Psi v>c shifts. More tidbits on it are found in the books by 1st 5th, 'Knights of Mars' and 'Star Script' for those interested in the Race experience and some theory.

USAF Pilots help train Iraqis Pilots

Authentic Q5 Leap Psi painting of the 900 LY distant Gomez Hamburger Galaxy; British Security detail

British Police with checkers on hat bands match to the RV floor of the Psi Painting; on Security Alert

(FMR) UK PM Tony Blair; Psi painting of finger signals (above, far right)

TIME LEAP 1st 5th

My mom Adeline Pearson/Griesbach, who is now deceased (left of center at back holding a little one) in a village in East Pakistan (Bangladesh), 1964, pre Jihad animosity. My father worked for the UN/ILO.

 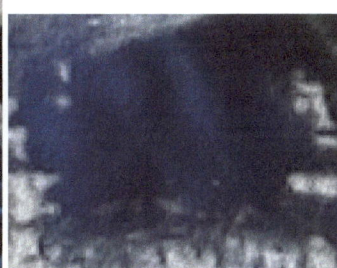 

Pakistan enemy radicals took last vote; Psi paint of the blue burka gang; marker for sharia/burkas

   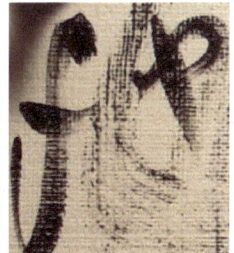 

Black burka with 'dark alien hand' gloves arrangement; 'Alien hand' from Jihad video July 20/09; RV burkas

Ft. Benning Army Rangers scaling wall; Delphi Oracle prophecy 'wooden walls'; Ranger's glove

TIME LEAP

Webbing - Afghanistan troops; remote viewing psychic painting of matching material

Iraq Aug 22, 2010 - Top Cmdr Gen Ray Odierno *striding* forwards; Scene from a 'Star Wars' episode, time-links to the Leap

Gen Odierno's group (you can make them out in front of the center bottom emote stick-figure) was striding, like the Ranger in *Lord of the Rings* by JRR Tolkien was called Strider, too; modern high tech helmet & psi paint (above, right)

TIME LEAP

Marine Commandant Gen. James Conway

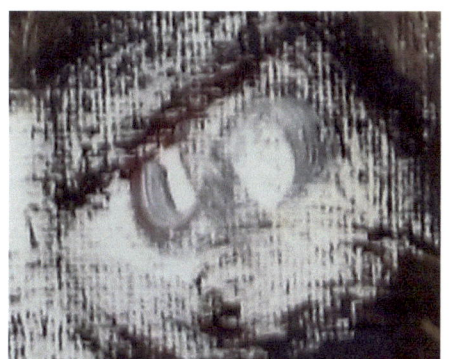  

Q5 Leap emote of Gen. Conway/knuckles visual /round plaque visual at right & braid, at far left for the Marines crest

 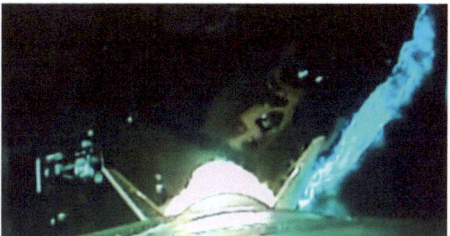 

'Starfire' - Q5 Leap Psi Paint 1983 by 1st 5th; Shuttle photo looking down to Earth, One of First computer confirmed beyond any possibility of being refuted, Q5 Leap *Precognitive* Psi Painting Remote Views (right)

Clint Eastwood - 'Heartbreak Ridge' Q5 Leap hats
Note the Conquistador helmet glimpse, descriptive visual - the Marines took the Ridge

Oct 6, 2010 Medal of Honor presented posthumously to 24 yr old
Green Beret Staff Sgt. Robert Miller

Ambushed by 100 enemy combatants hiding behind boulders, he stayed in the kill zone and saved the lives of 22 men.   Jan 25, 2008 Kunar, Afghanistan

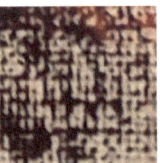

Green Beret, Staff Sgt Robert Miller, Psi painting image in bottom right corner

TIME LEAP

Medium sized Artillery Iraq 2010

Lt Gen Bob Cone, Iraq Deputy Commander, Aug 28, 2010

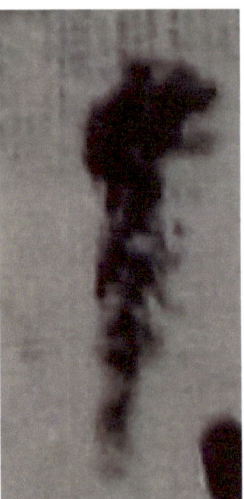

USA an emote visual depicting a row of troops with their guns in Iraq; close up of gun below, pointing down

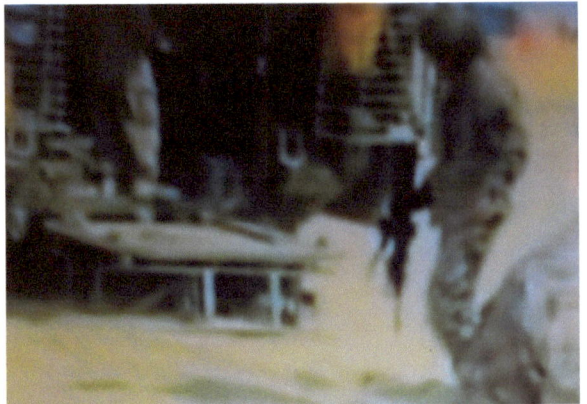

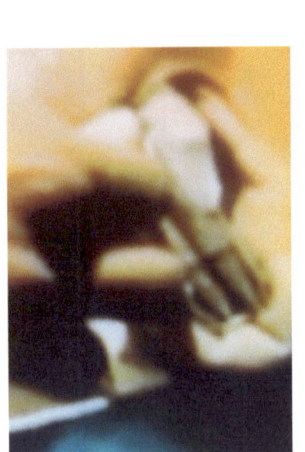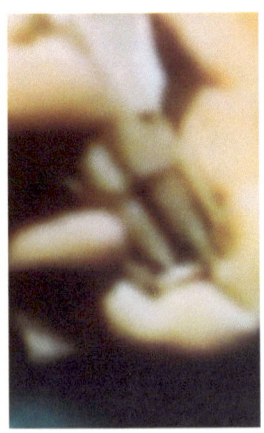

Aug 22- US troops Iraq - loading bullets and Q5 Leap RV

TIME LEAP 1ˢᵗ 5ᵗʰ

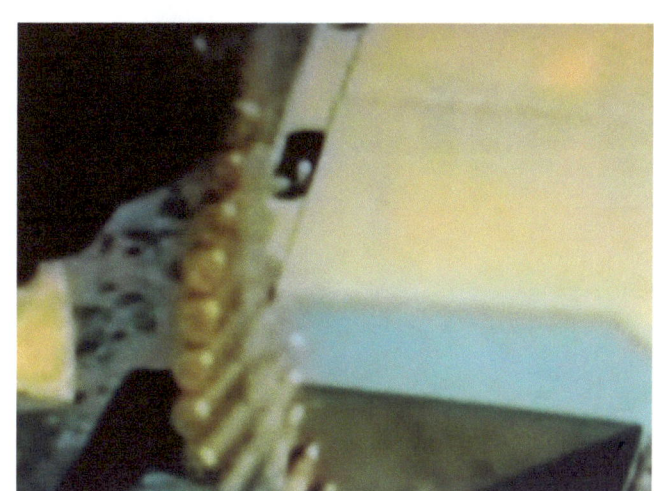

Bullets & Shot gun shell

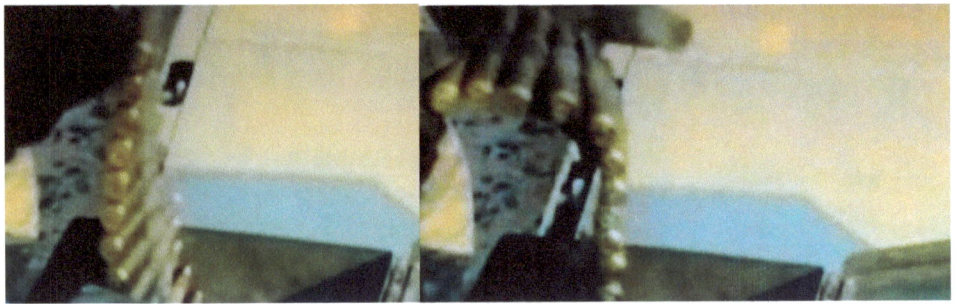

TIME LEAP

(1990s) Psi pencil drawing with the netting & bullet visuals

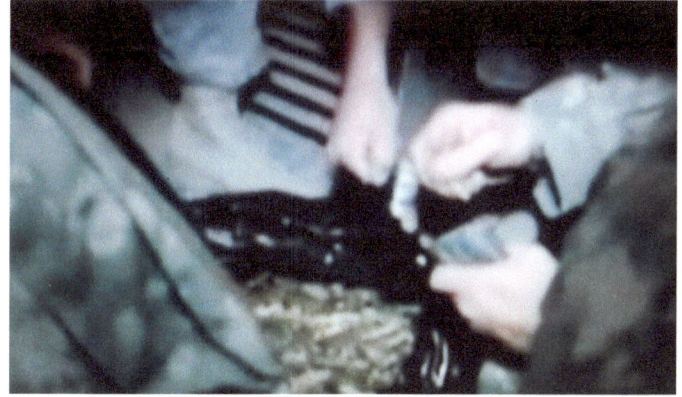

CF-18 Hornets, Edmonton Garrison, Alberta, Canada evening trails

CF-18 Hornet Jet Trails visuals

CF-18 Hornets jet trails over Q5 Leap for Sun Fire Ops by 1st 5th

Q5 Leap - Psi painting 3d - Canadian Parliament buildings Ottawa Ontario 2010
Terrorist round up in timely secure fashion Ottawa, Ont. Aug 26, 2010

General Bill Caldwell IV, Cmdr NATO training Mission Afghanistan 2010

Training Afghan Army arduous but rewarding process 2010

Afghan training large gun ~ Q5 Leap gun visual & emote

TIME LEAP

 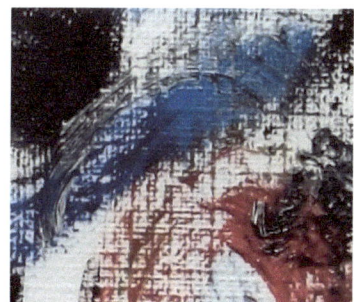 

Wild Blue Yonder - Army jet trail & Q5 Leap swoop visual match Aug 27, 2010; white trails

 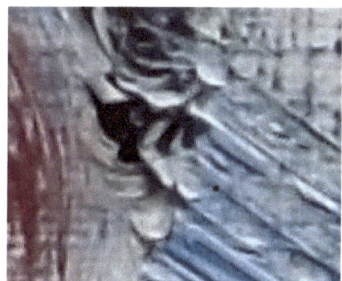 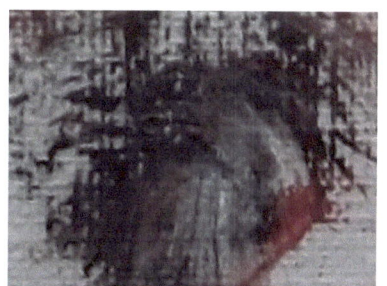

USAF Thunderbirds Aug 27, 2010

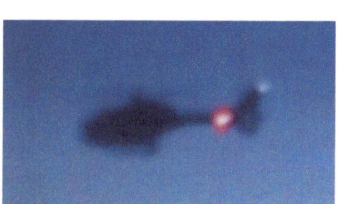 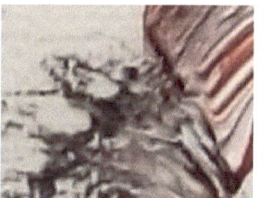  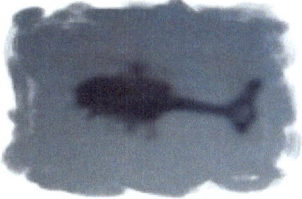

Edmonton, Alberta Police Chopper with 'small fish' descriptive visual emotes

TIME LEAP

Troops with Q5 Leap Psi paints of helmets and front of vehicle

USA soldier - Q5 Leap psi painting of Gun with white dots marker visual Iraq 2010

Covered vehicles leaving Iraq after a successful Operation Iraqi Freedom Aug 28, 2010

TIME LEAP

Rare CF-18 crash with Pilot bailing in the nick of time, Lethbridge, AB

Edmonton Garrison former designation 'Griesbach for Maj Gen W. A. Griesbach, son of the first man to sign up for the North West Mounted Police, now known of course as the RCMP, Royal Canadian Police' Tomb of the unknown soldier bottom left: RCMP swearing in of the new Gov Gen of Canada, D. Johnston

Otter new to the Zoo, Edmonton, AB

 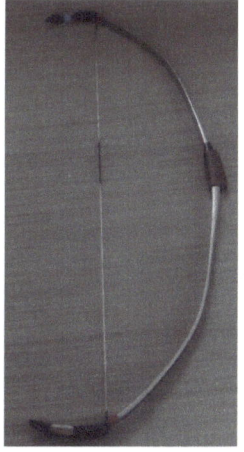 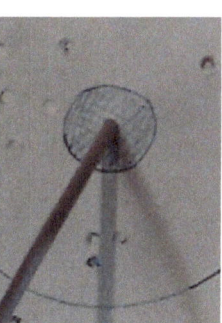

Chariot excerpt - bragging about proficiency too, doing it behind your back as well as describing the other actuality of bow and arrows' days, the strikes behind the back and the necessity of removing it (see next page); Kaya bow's Bulls eye dead center shot

The arm behind the back visual (in 'The Mummy Returns')was the match to the above Chariot manoeuvring. The hand being behind the back was also very descriptive as a marker and tale of the reality of bow and arrow days, the uncommon position for shooting and the common position for being shot in the back and reaching back…for the arrow. Common to bow and arrow days. Descriptive of actualities. 'getting shot in the back' warnings…built in as a function of an Oracle. More insider chat on the actual nature the internal workings of the Oracle. Intricate dimensions. Stillness and motion. The freeze point …and the fluidity and necessity of motion inherent to achieve a Leap. There is no a to b without motion. Even in Q5 Leap there is repositioning. If not strictly linear in nature…in how it is done. There is still that basic linear measure of point a and point b. distinguished as separate points. Parts of a whole. Different parts. Not a oneness. The division of space necessary for any a and b coordinates. Even with a Necker cube shift, the central point of directional totality, that leaps to a new repositioning. There is a built in assumed and measurable otherness to the points a and b. so motion is derived by division as much as by linear continuities. Timelines and Space Leaps are necessarily part of any division of here and there, or point a and point b. even point to point would be defined by right edge and center of point and the next left edge and center of point.

'EXPENDABLES' Stallone & Statham 2010

www.mapleconnection.com

'The Expendables' starring Sylvester Stallone; with matching Q5 Leap psi paint

  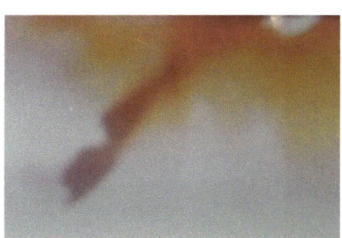 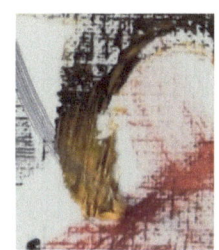

Sylvester Stallone and RV; Chopper blade with matching RV psi painting

'RAMBO' starring Sylvester Stallone; Q5 Leap psi paintings - BOW

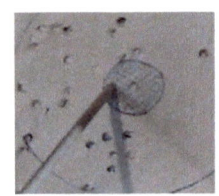

RV described 'hole in one' bullseye

CANADIAN SPECIAL OPS JULY 21, 2010

Q5 Leap Remote Viewing Psi paints of soldiers' faces...look for form and pattern
Edmonton Garrison soldiers Aug 11, 2010; green flat vehicle paint RV

TOXOPHILUS
THE FCHOLE OF FHOOTINGHE CONTEYNED IN TVVO BOOKES
By Roger Ascham, 1545

This book contains parts from both the 1864 Rev. Dr. Giles Edition as well as from the 1895 edition by Edward Arber.

- APOLOGIA
- CHRONICLE OF THE LIFE OF ROGER ASCHAM
- ORIGINAL INDEX
- THE ROYAL ARMS
- DEDICATION TO KING HENRY VIII
- TO ALL GENTLEMEN AND YEOMAN OF ENGLAND
- THE FIRST BOOK OF THE SCHOOL OF SHOOTING
- THE SECOND BOOK OF THE SCHOOL OF SHOOTING

 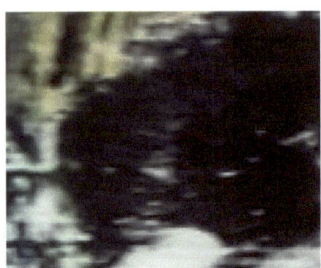

British Bobbies hat with Q5 Leap psi paint of View from back

 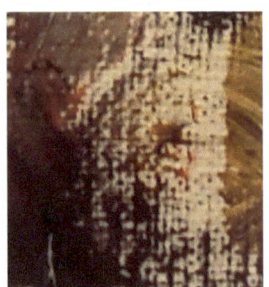

Q5 Leap - pig's visual Aug 23, 2010 - the cops like it....

Military troops - wet road and matching View Aug 13, 2010

Canadian Pilot 'Hurricane' fighter plane

Toronto, Ontario, Canada – OPP –

Hwy 401 car chase ends; stick emote

Ca Highway Patrol Aug 15, 2010

tire did it…

'Chariot' papyrus – Q5 Leap Star Trail quantum encoded Remote View

encapsulation. Currently being decoded and time linked.
See 'Ancient Links & Future Trails' for more details on this exciting discovery.

Measuring stick - ruler with notches; RV descriptive visual, also the feet and place marker for place to place again specifically implies distance that is actual.
Measure, the notches on that long strip over the horse in the chariot the horizontal looks like the bottom of a laptop not the screen upper one, measure e=mc squared c is distance light moving at a constant speed. Over a distance. Measured by speed and …so is light that is not moving, Dark? Just wondering. V=0 is that dark? For light? No light …implies motion is in LIGHT as a necessity. V>c…super luminous they call it. super luminous motion was supposedly exhibited here by an optical illusion. In keeping with the new confirmed discovery of psychic facility achievement with speeds greater than the known and measured speed of light, we likely need to apply new theory with the introduction of Psi v>c.

RV structure architecture, 'desktop pc' at Naqeh e Rostam, Iran ; excerpt from Chariot papyrus -bottom right corner - placed horizontally you can see a pc mouse and top of hand at it
NO BURNING THE WITCHES in 2010

Troops in Marjah, Afghanistan

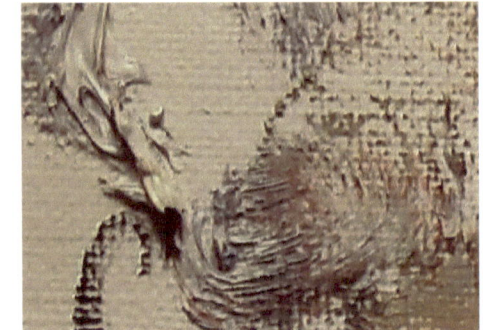

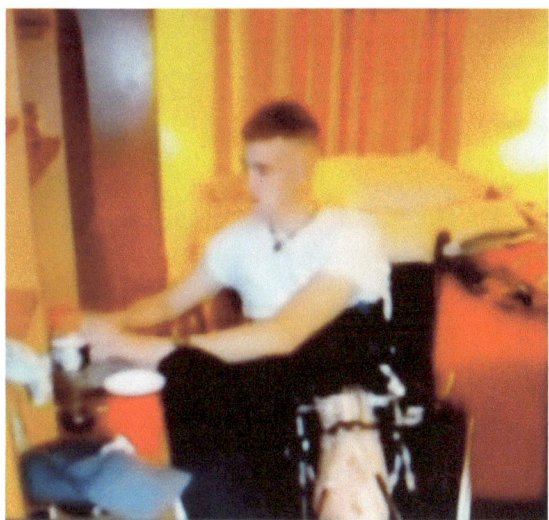  

Vet wounded warrior; Q5 leap matching RV; www.uso.org/giveback10 to pitch in

Here is the close up of the 'mop head' descriptive for the visual psi painting of the wounded vet above left, in AVATAR fashion you can see the arrow; as a bow Remote Viewing theme imagery, visual emote marker as the horizontal line on the cross shape above. We are hoping for a future Shadow Ops that would be manned by disciplined dedicated trained Psi Deepside/Earthside Quantum Leap adventurers.

 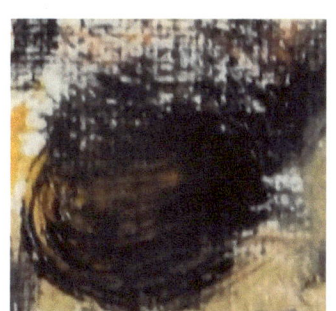 

'Mercury Rising' starring Bruce Willis; Q5 Leap of hat and brim visual emote

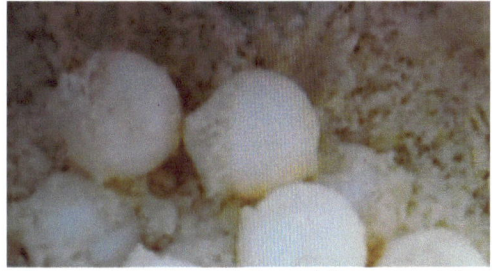   

Sea turtle eggs & Remote View; Seal flippers and dolphin fin (above, right)

Happy to -WIN- USA Troops leaving Iraq in successful conclusion to their mission to beat the bad guys and restore freedom!

1st 5th 's **idea**- *Covered tops- Applied and extended here on these wide vehicles*

TIME LEAP 1ˢᵗ 5ᵗʰ

Psi paint of troops' vehicles top cover *credit to 1ˢᵗ 5ᵗʰ*

YES IT WAS MY IDEA- CREDITED TO ME TO THE UNITED STATES MILITARY that is confirmed and not in question. It was my hammering at them for 14 hours on covering them over, when Gen P Pace and Gen Rumsfeld were still in. It wasn't easy it was akin to telling men to put their sweater on. I persisted to put it mildly and they covered up. Since then they openly acknowledged it to me directly via our contacts. It was likely a Ghost too, participating. I swore steady and I hadn't been, although they would find that hard to believe now. Gen Pace said it reminded him of an old now passed on War buddy. And here at the Open Stargate we do indeed get the odd Military Ghost passing by; it happens. I got them to agree to cover up, it was their own version of hobbit Ville that occurred as a result.

Troops Leaving Iraq Aug 2010, with 50,000 remaining; Q5 Leap of troops curving around

 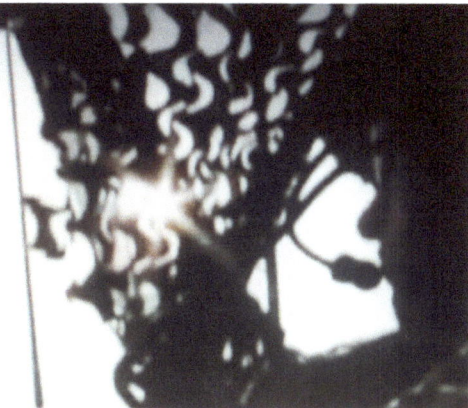

Close up- you can make out the hats of the curved rows of troops

Conditions are much improved -no Iraqis are forced to live indoors only these days, they got their land and their lives back. As for the radical die hards let us hope they're destined to die out eventually, there is too much good on this Planet.

Troops- leaving a successfully completed Operation Iraqi Freedom 2010

TIME LEAP

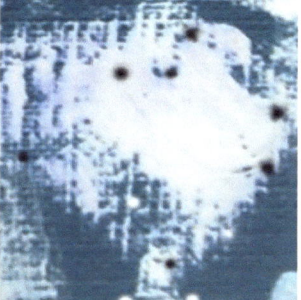

RV psi paint & pc negative image as an 'ape' in white dots; Psi paints often show overlapping themes in a given time frame, here is an image of a visually similar Military strike in Afghanistan; hand shadow 'wolf'

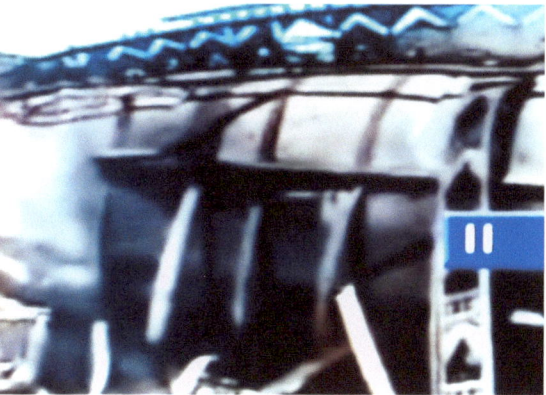

Photos re- Pilots supporting the ground troops in Afghan

TIME LEAP 1st 5th 58

'The Mummy Returns' starring- Brendan Fraser & John Hannah

'Mummy Returns' hand behind back pulling out an arrow; Chariot with hand back

 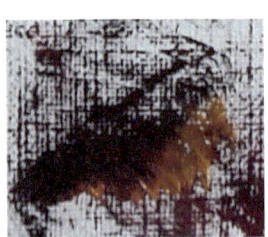 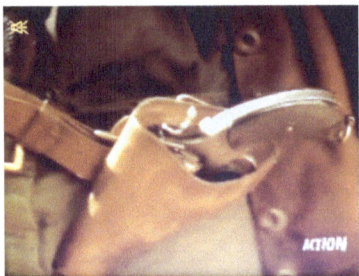 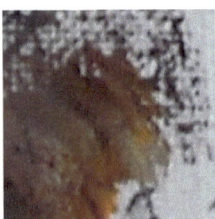

Remote Views - gun barrel & grip (below)

 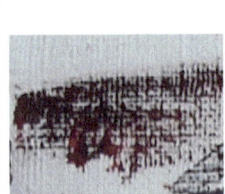  

Bullet crossed belts and matching 'bullet' with side marker visuals - if you look carefully inside the center of the image at right, above, you can make out a bullet.; Crossed blades

Knife blade; Q5 Leap Psi painting of blade and hilt visuals, (top right corner) dbl edging'; more Yemeni blades

TIME LEAP

'The Mummy Returns' selection of Bows Remote View (below)

 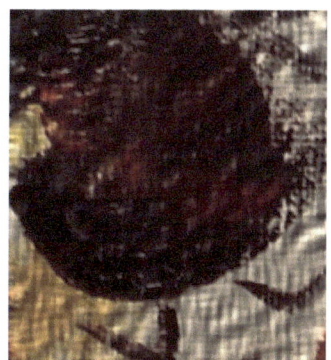 

Tom & Katie Cruise swirling skirt California dance RV; *Minority Report* eye'; *'MI:2'* leap'

God's sense of humour - a vacuum cleaner place is where I went to get that papyrus…free like me and Gideon's Bible. A 'prize' for going. I didn't have carpets to vacuum. It was the psi sense directing me, drawing me to it. The necessity or a certain/future event. I went because it was so. Meant to be, in a new additional dimensional linking up of my self and the ancient Master's Remote Viewing encapsulation. Also, the modern descriptive of a 'vacuum' coming into play with the overlapping timely theme of the NASA links with a jpl fax daily, during training years, albeit training of my Psi by the Military on the computer, with visual pixel release. A gruelling process not for the faint of heart. Uncanny precision in terms of the necessity of the act and the actual spontaneous achievement of it. The coming together of the two sides of that coin. Hard to believe it happened it was just so *odd.* And extremely typical in terms of the surfacing and linking timely relevancy of the Remote Viewing hieroglyphic arrangements, the what I term- encapsulations. It was indeed meant to be. It was a realization of a dream the opening codes of the Star Trail …a quantum door, trail and map…the key is…our understanding as well as the time factor. The meaning is revealed with a time key. In it's own timeliness we know what it is pointing out and describing. A time piece. Like a watch. Kinda. A watch-key.

Another dimensionality at play …like the difference between a 2d jigsaw puzzle and a Rubick's cube…this one opens and things click into place with the extra dimensionality of Time Leaps. Achievable by Quantum 5th. It is not just the usual linear dimension of time as in doing a puzzle either of those examples as time goes by …it's not oh look how long it took to do it. It's not linear realization or measure. It's a leap that involves time line links this time to that, both forwards and backwards. Not limited to forwards only present to future realization of events and moments. Leaping involves the components of Space Light and Time Light as already set out by our confirmation of the Psi Race both in real time for space leap and the time leap of the precog painting done by psi years earlier.

Edmonton, Alberta glorious sky trails

'I Spy' starring Owen Wilson & Eddie Murphy

Stealth ship from 'I Spy' with Q5 Leap psi paintings

Stealth ship diagonal outlined bottom left to upper right

TIME LEAP 1st 5th 62

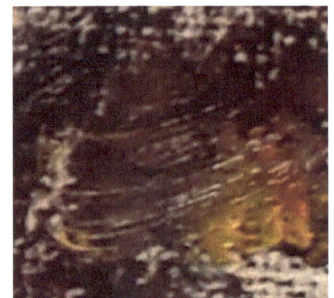

Owen Wilson in the ship facing forwards; matching 'head' in Psi painting; Stealth emote

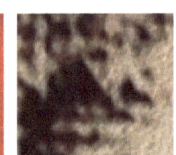

George Clooney the star talent, presenting a slightly modified version of what happens in the movie 'Men Who Stare At Goats' - 1983 Fort Bragg, US Army Intelligence; F-35 Stealth craft (above, right) RV of Canadian purchase of Stealth 2010

TIME LEAP

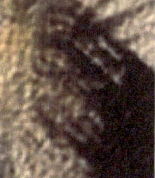

Afghan 2010- looking into the ditch'; RV 2nd 5th 'JJ mcQuay (Open Stargate's *Anderson*)

Q5 Leap of Ditch; Special Ops images, Iraq

Fighting for FREEDOM   ....the SPECIAL OPS in Iraq 2010

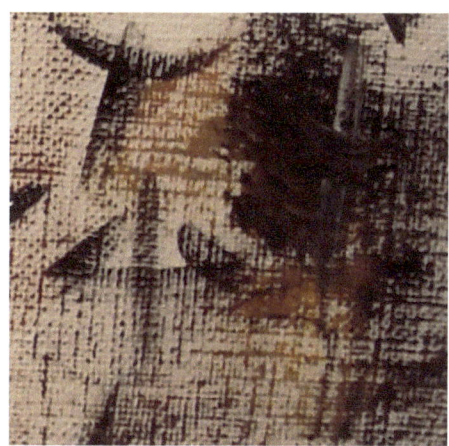

TIME LEAP

Col Oliver North, with SWAT team in Iraq 2010; Q5 Leap emote visual for SWAT

Lt Col John Prairie; matching Q5 leap Psi painting (above, right)

Gen Radi Mohammad

  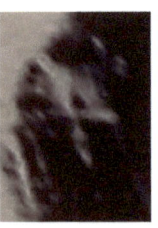

Gen Barwari

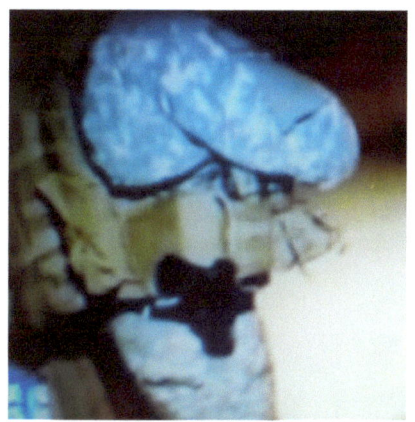 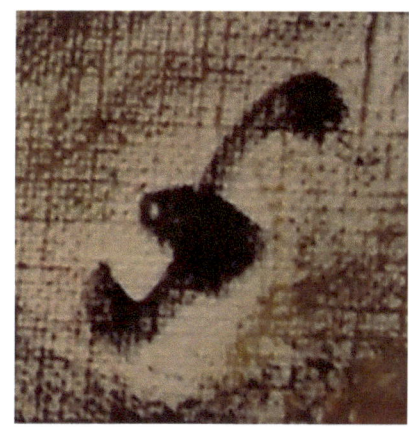 

Gun at side with matching remote view Psi painting

 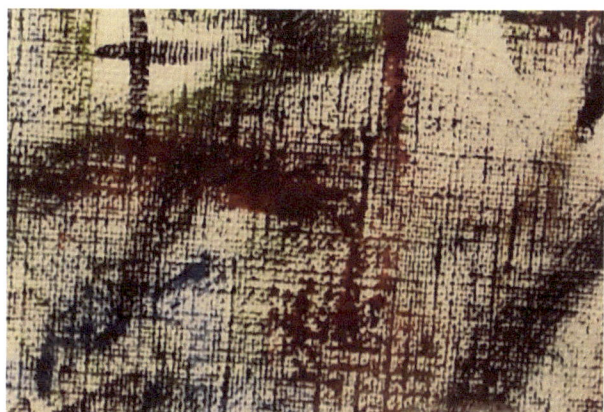

Gun barrel in brownish tones; note the 'face' descriptive visual in the pattern Recognition of the Psi painting at right, very typical of Remote View paints; And the emote for 'flying' as he was moving fast (below, left); Knight's visor visual RV painting of the helmet crease

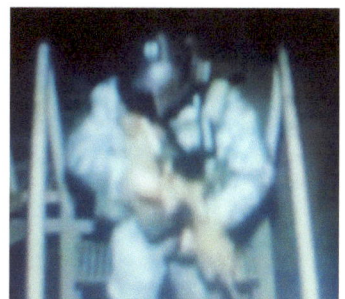 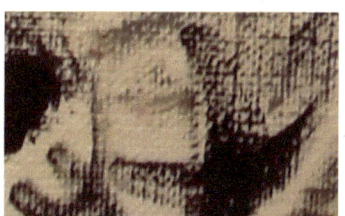 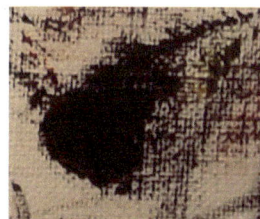 

Visor style metal helmet like a Knight's RV visual; Hieroglyph for Grey Night

End of combat actions in Iraq Aug 31, 2010; Col Oliver North (Fox - 'War Stories') with SWAT members; Special Ops teams remaining to assist with security in Iraq; Q5 Leap Psi gladly continuing as well.

Note the hand up at top right corner in the Chariot View frame at the left, a precision match to the left top corner of the photo of the men catching their rifles tossed into the air at the Twilight Tattoo; gun lengths in between dots; (below) RV of June 28, 2008

Twirling of the guns and the flash of the knives on the ends, by the 3rd Infantry Regiment, the American Military's honour guard, at the yearly 'Twilight Tattoo'. I can see the guns' and knives' theme in the Chariot piece now. The hieroglyphs presenting as multi-faceted as ever, the gun in the lower left corner, is also a dog's 'tail', representing their 'tale'. Geraldo Rivera, (Fox Cable News) at the front.

Geraldo & wife, 2010

'Dirty Harry' starring Clint Eastwood

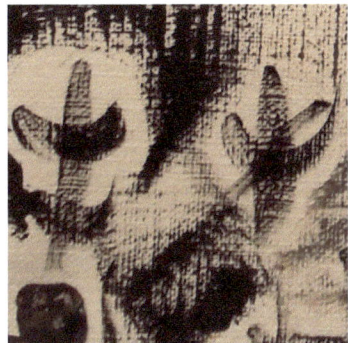

Gun barrel and at left the knife in the emote hand, Harry stabbed the bad guy with; bullet casing from start of the movie, note RV emote also holding it. An Ace RV (below, right); RV of 'witches' broom (left)

& *the Wizard* Col Oliver North I presume, time linking to an Edmonton, Alberta splendid Jet Trail on his Birthday, Oct 7, 2010. Well, they can't bake me as a Witch when their own Fox Birthday has the Wizard of Fox *War Stories* on the Star Trail time synched IN.

TIME LEAP

American East Coast -Witchcraft Act passed in 1541-
"thou shalt not suffer a witch to live"
-death penalty ended in 1735.
Last person convicted was Jane Rebecca Yorke, a medium who was fined 5 lbs for claiming to be able to contact dead service men in 1944.

Afghan Special Ops training - orange door

Special Ops forces' dog's ears and matching RV

TIME LEAP

'Babylon A.D.' starring Vin Diesel

Emotes for 'Leap'; Edmonton, Alberta, Canadian cops own *Teleport Leap* emote

Gideon's Bible (page 224)
Judges Chapter 7
"7:18 When I blow with a trumpet, I and all that are with me, then blow ye the trumpets also on every side of all the camp, and say, The sword of the LORD and of Gideon."
Here I will read about Gideon's Sword moment and go see if I can tune in to paint it but we won't have a photo so you just have to look for it.
Aimed time tunnelling….might as well. Call it Sphinx …it's EXP PSI
Pretty sure that part is already in the one book about making the distinction between the ones who got down to lap up the water and the ones who had the water raised up to their mouths with their hands. The ones who acted like beasts compared to the ones using tools concepts, water in cupped hands. Cups. The Holy Grail was to cup your hand for water. That's the Grail descriptive on that page 225. Gideon's Sword …fine line shit. The practice of discernment for future certain, is how I see it. Selection of the most advancing. Not just all here all same ugh.
Yeah ok it was the LORD gave Gideon the Sword, it was Gideon's and the LORD'S Sword. See. It was Gideon's Sword but it was the LORD'S sword. He gets the Life and Death decisions, that's just how it is. Even with the RV that's just how it is. We don't control the forces of life and death we truly don't. it's not ours to deal. Every one of us dies and we don't know when. I think those are basic reality conditions. And a caution there of a sorts to remember that. It's up to the LORD to play out our Gideon's Sword. Earth 2010 could be interesting. In the 1980s I viewed - 0 point 1 2 -dot was not a decimal, explained out as an in between., you know how they actually did the web about ten years later. The www. It was the dot. I called it point it was the dot. I had it all explained out to keep things open ended you would do like 'rain . Falls' so the time frame was flexible. A dot, not a decimal, that 0 1 dot 2 is how we would read it now. An RV marker for the internet connection mode. A digital gap leap of faith.

TIME LEAP

USA Chairman of the Joint Chiefs of Staff, Adm. Mullen; Cmdr Frank Castelano (USS Bainbridge) rescued Capt. Richard Phillips from Pirates off Somalia, of Ship Maersk Alabama. (above, at right in photo)

Q5 Leap Psi paintings by 1st 5th of the US Navy SEAL Team VI, April 9, 2009 - 3 simultaneous shots taking out Somalian Pirates off the West Coast of Africa. (Below, left) long shot visual Pre-Cog paint with '3' as cuffs, match to SEAL Team 6 truly amazing display of synchronicity when shooting the Pirates and rescuing Cap't Phillips. Navy Seals aboard the USS Bainbridge rescued the brave unarmed merchant marine Capt. Phillips who was taken as a voluntary hostage to spare his crew. The USA sent 3 destroyers in. 3 Pirates were shot simultaneously, and one was captured. Next photo below with it's RV is a flipper entangled in mesh ladder, a view 'landmark' match to Canadian Warship Winnipeg fighting Pirates a few days later, in the same area, as the rescue ops.

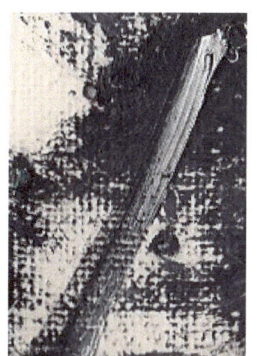
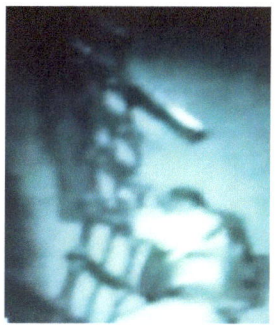
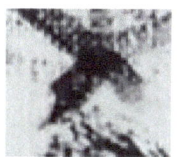

Remarkable precision remote view psychic Pre-Cog paint prior to SEAL Team VI shooting 3 Pirates.; RV flipper and ladder, Warship Winnipeg marker in the same area, fighting Pirates in the same time frame.

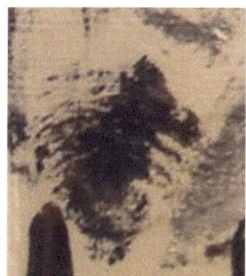
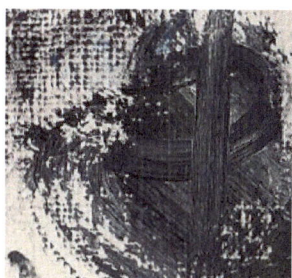

US Navy SEALS swimming with guns, and the matching visual remote view painting & emote.

Leap Visual - 'Last Crusades' starring Harrison Ford
visual imagery Quantum SpaceTimeLight-encoded, Q5 Leap

MEDAL of HONOR - Living recipient:
Staff Sergeant Salvatore Guinta currently stationed in Italy

Former Army Specialist when he bravely responded in battle, to rescue others, 2007.

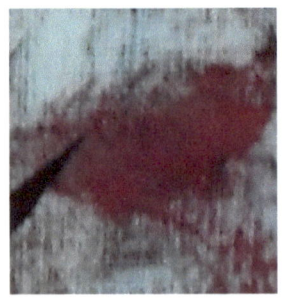

TIME LEAP 1st 5th

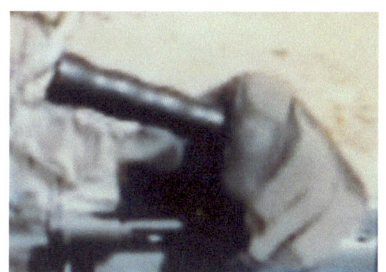

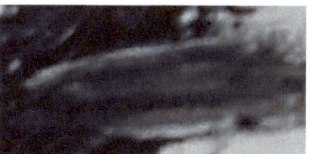

Afghanistan, 2010 - Gun tip and glove RV paints

USA Marines Afghanistan - RV of gun barrels

Throwing - Q5 leap Psi paints formed emotes and descriptive visuals

 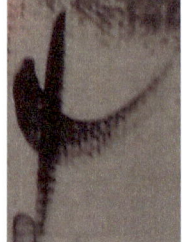  

Q5 Leap began as Mars Reconnaissance- 'nailed to the front' emotes; My wish kitty 'Puddingtons' courtesy of Edmonton Garrison, Alberta, Canada; Star Trail One by 1st 5th; Puddingtons' endorsement; (below, right) the emote for the Canadian troops in Afghanistan

TIME LEAP

Troops Afghanistan Aug 16, 2010 large 'Stargate Door' Q5 Leap theme ; Naqeh-e-Rostam, Iran, Earth

Potential for future Star Trail links with the door theme imagery matching Naqsh-e Rostam, Iran ancient RV

Plunging

  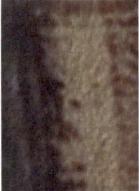

Chmn Joint Chiefs of Staff, Adm Mike Mullen (above, left); RV of tan cap; vehicle/antennae visuals

Hor Em Akhet (below) also symbolizes the Sphinx. See how the top round red is on it and under the space flight looking ship. *Raiders of the Lost Ark* starring Harrison Ford used *Horus* with the two dogs; Anubis stood for the Future. I used it for the First Viewer of Jupiter's marker. A dingo is an Aussie dog. The original CRV coordinate remote viewer of the CIA Project Stargate (this is *Open Stargate*) was the first viewer of JUPITER. RV, as red dot on Jupiter.

RV 1980s; St. Glass by 1st 5th of 'Hor Em Akhet' -Horus On the Horizon, a Sphinx marker; excerpt Ramses II, Valley of Kings, note the same round red object underneath

Ramses II ; Star Trail decoding from Chariot papyrus (see 'Star Script' by 1st 5th for info on method)

   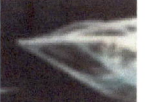

M86 Virgo Cluster (APOD photo); 'Canaliens' Psi paint by 1st 5th

A good volcano smoke from space (Earth Observatory, Astronaut photos) plume, to match with the plumes on the Chariot's horses head gear visually describing the white plumage of the View theme.

TIME LEAP

Sept 18, 2010 Pope Benedict XVI and Queen Elizabeth II - synchronized to *Chariot*

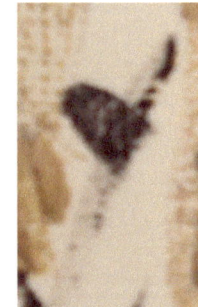

Bow tip

Side emote

TIME LEAP

Pope Benedict XVI, Queen Elizabeth II & Prince Charles

  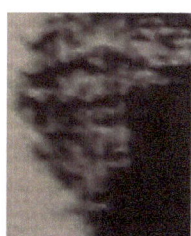

Prince Charles & Cdn Navy, Sword Emote ; Pope Benedict XVI & Prince Charles, with RV visual of Prince

Pope Benedict XVI raised Cross, RV umbrella descriptive RV for raised; Cross & emote

   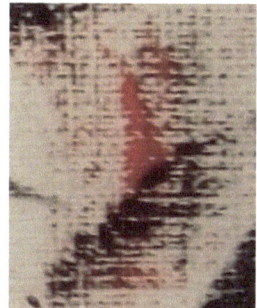

Pope Benedict XVI with Cross sideways and red inner lining visual

TIME LEAP

  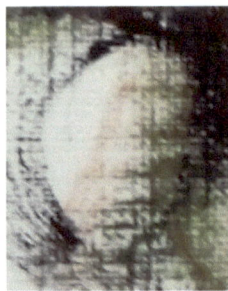 

Yemen red splotch on ground; Q5 leap of 'I Robot' starring Will Smith (Fusion center's look alike)

Chopper Edmonton, Alberta, Canada; chopper emotes

 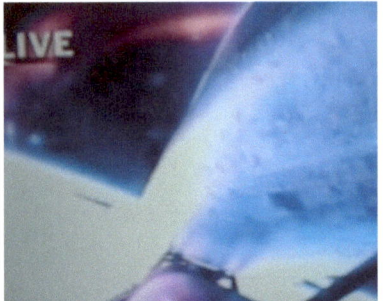 

Q5 Leap Feb 19, 2006 ship; NASA Shuttle Discovery launch Feb 07, 2008

 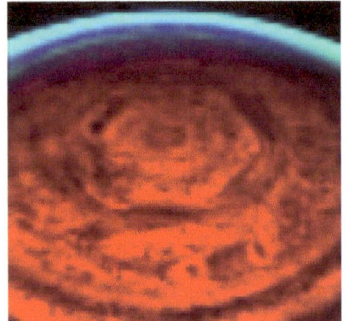 

Q5 Leap Star Ship; Saturn, N. Pole (NASA photo); 'Stealth' movie clip like the Shuttle's light effect

(Fmr) CIA Director Michael Hayden – hand signalling to 1st 5th with corresponding Q5 Leap Psi painting; stick-figure black *emote* is 'signalling' descriptive of Spy chat

Broward Cty Miami – Police perfect pit manoeuvre and suspects subdued Sept 22/2010

NATO troops Afghan Sept 20, 2010

Vertical bullets

ISAF (International Security Assistance Forces) Afghan 2010

TIME LEAP

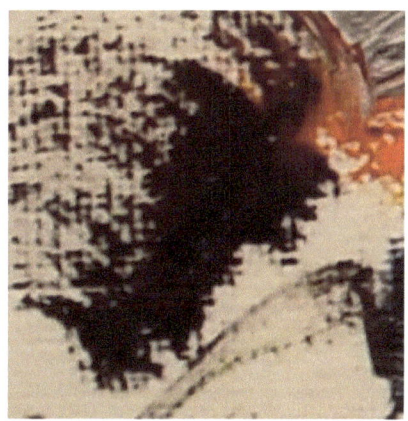

Top Cmdr Afghan 2010, Gen David H. Petraeus with matching aced Remote View; Baghdad 2006
Gen Petraeus orchestrated the successful Surge that won the Iraqis their Peace & Freedom

TIME LEAP 1st 5th 84

'First Blood' starring Sylvester Stallone

 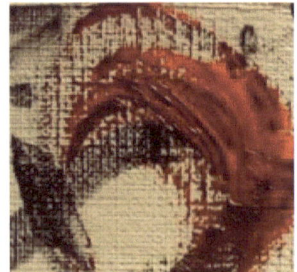   

Bow excerpt; RCMP musical Ride flags RV; assortment of RV bow emotes

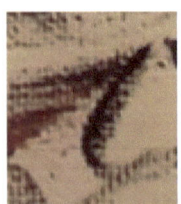  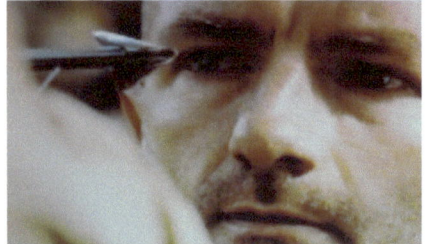 

'Rambo' starring Sylvester Stallone; arrow tip RV

West Bank, Israel; 'Chambers' Q5 Leap psi painting by 1st 5th oil/canvas 16"x20"

Gideon's Bible (page 384)   II Chronicles Chapter 5
3:17 "And the priests that bare the ark of the covenant of the LORD stood firm on dry ground in the midst of Jordan and all the Israelites passed over on dry land, until all the people were passed clean over Jordan."

According to the Bible story where Moses parted the Red Sea and the scientists finding perhaps that it was further along in location, where a known weather wind phenomenon may have occurred to push the waters back and give them a brief period of dryland. The Arc is also in the Bible as accounting for Dryland. The arc/oracle would be them finding the right timing for such a phenomenon to be useful for them to use it to go for their freedom. That's not just plain 'luck' as such. Not if it was the Oracle providing them the specifics that led to their deliverance. That is still *divine intervention* if it was Q5 Leap like Quantum tuning in their own Viewing intuitions that led them to it…at the right TIME for timing, place and time, not luck, quantum tuning, precision …on the right path at the right time for survival is part of what this is all about.
It's what it's for. And why they used Oracles not for love potions or weather forecasts. It was to lead to favourable outcomes in terms of the life and death situations, like battles which is why it is showing as so developed and linked into those situations so often and also so precisely. That's diving intervention. It's God's outcome, life or death. We don't control it everyone dies. And it's timing and place specific. I had the parting of the sea as finding dryland. Same deal, that weather phenomenon that pushed the water aside, it was up to them to be there for it, or to know. However they did it, it was time and place, if it was a viewer leap then it was still linking to the greater certain/future. That's what we would call divine providence. Not 'luck' this Q5 Leap /prophecy/oracle is not a gambling luck thing. We are finding it to have it's own reasonable methodology it's own brand of consistency like the Quantum level that particle physicists are studying with photographic evidence at those large haldron particle accelerators. It's not speculation. They have names for the different quantum particles according to behaviour and character. They're very 'real' it's Physics. At atomic and quantum levels. It's not 'luck' …it's quantum. You could say they were lucky to have the quantum. Like, lucky to have fields of crops to eat. They were planted grew and harvested for food. It wasn't luck…but they were *fortunate* as in good fortune. It turned out well. The results were good. In the I Ching they have

good outcomes, good fortune. It's an Oracle thing. But it's not a gamble, it's not 'sheer luck' like that, without substance. There is a physical reality as real as those crops in the field. With the same amount of order to it. We don't just pretend here. There is a system. Like when I do the Star Map I use certain specific outlined procedure. I follow it. Along with the psi links for timing etc. there is a formal system to it. Some of it is in Star Script, and other parts more developed as it goes along, in Ancient Links & Future Trails and ongoing. We are discovering it as we work it. Their model is rather silly but the water parting could have been a phenomenon. For sure, we get micro bursts up here strong excessive winds that come down from the Arctic …it was radically different that long ago any combination of factors was possible up to and including a direct hand from God other than the manner I already said, that it was all here on Earth under his direction as God is the overriding condition in a Universe that is not Godless and chaotic. There is divine planning that goes beyond our knowledge and experience. The fact we learn and discover pretty much shows that to be the basis of the Universe as we understand that. It's why we explore. Or the people would still be in the same static positioning that they were in since mankind was conceived.

Of course given the extent of our Universe left to explore and knowledge to attain, it is also possible that it was Aliens zapping him a route from on their anti-gravity platforms at too great a height for them to be seen but that's just one other possibility.

The focus here was on the idea of it having been a rare but entirely possible wind event that caused the dryland effect at a position that was ripe for it, and Moses leading his people as described in Exodus and also see II Chronicles V for reference, in the Bible (*Gideon's* page 384), to safety over dryland formed by a parting of waters.

In their model (study of Exodus/Moses by Center for Atmospheric Research, Boulder Colorado, USA and published in Public Library of Science Journal - PLoS ONE) they used the notion of winds blowing overnight, for example. They know no such thing. It could just as easily been a strong blast that lasted much briefer more focused and narrower in effects. As for the cause, the idea of extreme and unusual weather with winds being the main factor is entirely possible on this Planet. Especially with the raw state of the Planet, not being cluttered with the effects of population such as we see it today. Winds and/or other conditions as an anomaly but still natural. Albeit with some divine guidance, and that's of course where the quantum Viewing factor would have come into play for them to use with such precision oriented timing, and for such certain-future purpose as is the nature of prophecy and Oracle guidance, in particular.

  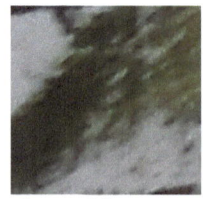 

Parting the Red Sea by 1st 5th; 2010 RV of Exodus; West Bank, enlarged from upper right of Exodus RV

British Constables on Security Alert Oct, 2010

Aliens in pubs evokes images of *Star Wars* movie, starring Harrison Ford. A pub scene with a variety of experienced Inter-Galactic travellers and sojourners, means to stay at a place for a time also known as wayfarers. And MIB will Smith and Jones. The white guy what's his name, oh Tommy Lee Jones. The middle name marker. Tommy the pinball wizard. Another one of the I Am the LORD's jokes …like the Orackle and the vacuum cleaner sales place. I didn't have carpet and I wasn't going to Egypt in particular at the time and why would I go get a free papyrus from Egypt for consulting a vacuum cleaner place? I did it from reading it in the paper. Buy I didn`t have carpet and I told them so. Still, they gave it to me for going for one the guy was over in Egypt. It was the priceless `Chariot` papyrus we use for the Q5 Leap decoding of the Star Trails. All it required to achieve this stupendous feat of precision Viewed retrieval was love of other culture, of humanity as a whole. Truly fulfilling the quest of the *5th Element.* Breathing fresh air into our adventure trail. A deed achieved because this unknown man was sharing. These are the little built in tests of faith that Last Crusade Holy Grail moment the leaps of faith they had 3 in that movie. They may be REAL. Whoever wrote that was looking up old Grail literature some of those early English books have some interesting tidbits it was no doubt passed along over the years many years a long time span is the descriptive. They were likely Viewing like the Early Egyptian Viewers there is more than one way to share an encapsulation. They used engravings back then. Deepside the longer back the further ahead. That's the Bow descriptive in Rambo the large man would have a longer range for that arrow. An authentic bullwhip taking a weapon. Harrison Ford, also the star of Star Wars, did repeats in his movies. He had that bullwhip taking their gun. For equality, on the side of that chariot carriage. That's a whip. They used whips. That spiral is our galaxies too. Taking Deepside as one descriptive. And using a whip. They use that in space travel already too, use a close to the planets effect to get them whipped out there, acceleration and gravity curves…you do NOT go in a straight line from one planet to another. Einstein. Space is curved and that's a fact. Technically Kepler only did curved lines Orbits, in space. It was Einstein filled it out, and it became curved Space. They would not have shit on Mars if they were still going a to b linear. We are far past linear modes already. You need to look it up if that fact escapes you. They curve them curling them round to get them to another planet the routes are not straight lines. Like Arrows and other projectiles there is a natural curve to things that comes into account. So bow your model of the universe. And that's how you do a Star Trail.

I am not including any of the female stars. None. Not one. No exceptions. Someone else can. I am sticking to the men. With all the men I watch over and with an older lady`s sensibilities. Doing this is like *water water everywhere nor any a drop to drink*. I learned that poem when I was young to write a test. It was a total recall memory test and I read it before I went in and I aced it. I actually forget how many pages, but even one blows me away now to remember I did that. It was one of those RV moments things has them. Like the Mar`s Claim Rock that many years later. Same rock on mars. (You have to read `Remote Viewing: Knights of Mars` for the actual as close to it as you`re getting account of how that happened.) It's got a lot of rocks. And I nailed the scenery around it precisely years later. Mars was a time light and space light leap…a combo.

Very proud of that achievement it took years to train for it. I think the Aliens glitches your Rover so I could do it. They held it…like you put your hand up in front of one of those crank toys…hold on a bit, this one is taken. I already had Mars and they gave it to me. That must be a validated |Claim in the Future so the Knights of Mars are very Real. Which is only cool too. We need our incentives like that on Earth. It keeps us adventurers satisfied. It's not all just life and death. We get to adventure explore …the one hieroglyph from ancient times was an Explorer. If you're not into Exploring you would not be going into Space. Exp for exploration and experience. This is not Court world you go play in your own corners over there. We don't have to Prove everything it's not snake eyes and dice rolls. It's not snakes and ladders. We don't have to prove something to enjoy or explore it.

Actual space debris asteroids hit Jupiter with large explosions. Astronomical in size. Easily visible. Seems creativity is not all entertainment. Some RV is time linked to surface messages; useful light info packets. Kind of like floating bubble holograms.

Old grainy film clip of nuclear explosion; still photo from video clip with vertical 'marks' on it

American Military (Fmr) Officers have stated publicly, Sept 2010 that there is evidence regarding incidents when Aliens intervened to prevent nuke tests; Spyland's MIB

TIME LEAP
1st 5th
89

Maj Gen Campbell, Afghanistan 2010; Q5 Leap psi paint of the diamond shape inbetween the stars on the American flag - the original spectacular achievement, the *Remote View of Jupiter in 1973* by the viewer of Stargate fame, was also a *reversed color field quantum effect*. He showed it to me on my training fax from Mars Reconnaisance, jpl/nasa/gov in 2007 one time, during secret Shadow Ops days

End Time Angel by 1st 5th; Jupiter Psi painting by 1st 5th, oil/linseed oil on paper Monochrome oddity Match to the Bubble Nebulae (below, right) NGC 7635

Jupiter, Auroras at Poles (Hubble Heritage photos); note the large *Jaws* starring Richard Dreyfuss, moment in the Chariot 'visual (above, right) The Orb was the First Remote View of Jupiter (too).

TIME LEAP   1st 5th   90

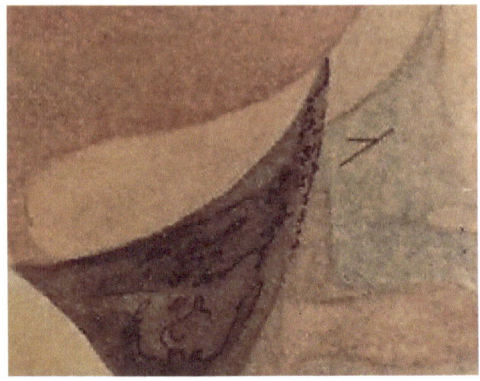 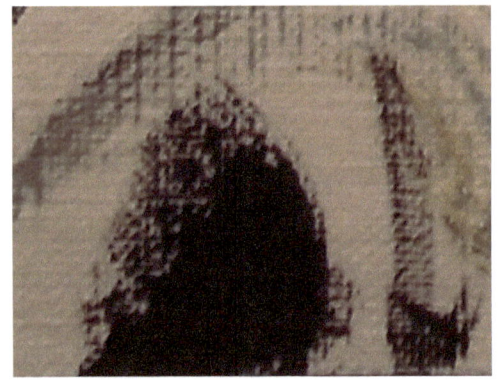 

Enlarged from Psi paint previous page, match to Troops in Afghan photo below, the erratic vertical squiggling, and overall 'like a shark's tooth' visual shape RV descriptive; enlarged from in the Psi paint above of the dark shark tooth, is the matching Q5 leap of the guns very small, but a lot of Quantum psi painting is. There is a sense to them, a cohesive unit very holistic in nature.

 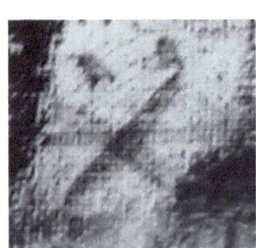

Jet trails emote

 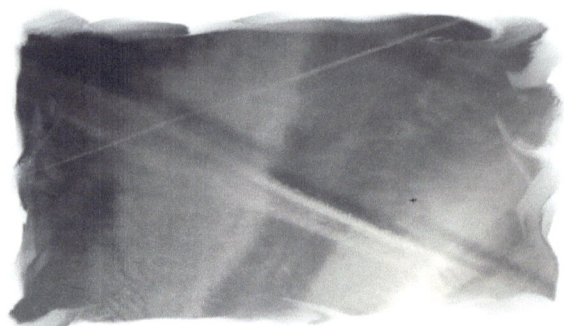

Troops in Afghanistan under Maj Gen Campbell; CF-18 Hornet Jet trails & emotes over Q5 Leap

  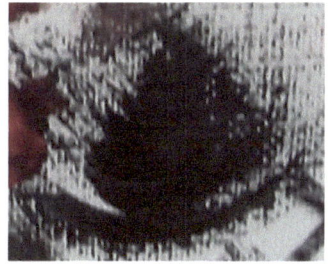

Raw Deal starring CA Gov A. Schwarzenegger, another rare RV find by local beat cops; RV of gun/bat; Chariot Papyrus, Giza pyramids; 3D of Pyramid with round-corners, RV

You do not have to prove everything, Earth is not Court World. We use discernment and knowledge to advance. Life consists of adventure too, not just Law. Remote Viewing requires Psychic and Creative talent as well as discipline and skill. You do not 'prove' either, you experience them and enjoy them. That said, there is a great deal more to the Remote Viewing in Shadow ops it's a security function. Surfaced here is some RV for your enjoyment. Fascinating as it is, it's not all we do or accomplish. There is a team working this, decoding as well as applying the remote streaming paints and scripting; Security and 'other'....

 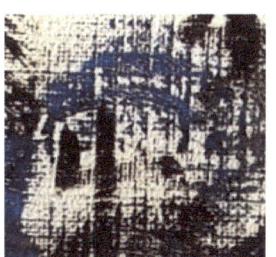  

Postman & remote view paint of him doing 'night crow' calls

 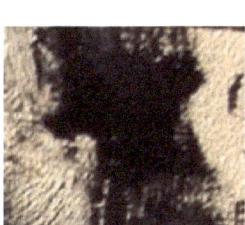  

HMCS Athabaska Operation Desert Storm 1990; Crows nest RV, Q5 Leap's 1st 5th is ON it

TIME LEAP

V sky trail and (quantum levels) small but distinguishable v in the corresponding psi paint

Special Fly over Q5 Leap Shadow Ops - Oct 6, 2010 - note the **red Canadian Maple Leaf** on tail

Arc Sky trail & psi paint

TIME LEAP 1st 5th 93

Pegasus flash 1st Airborne Division UK, Constable

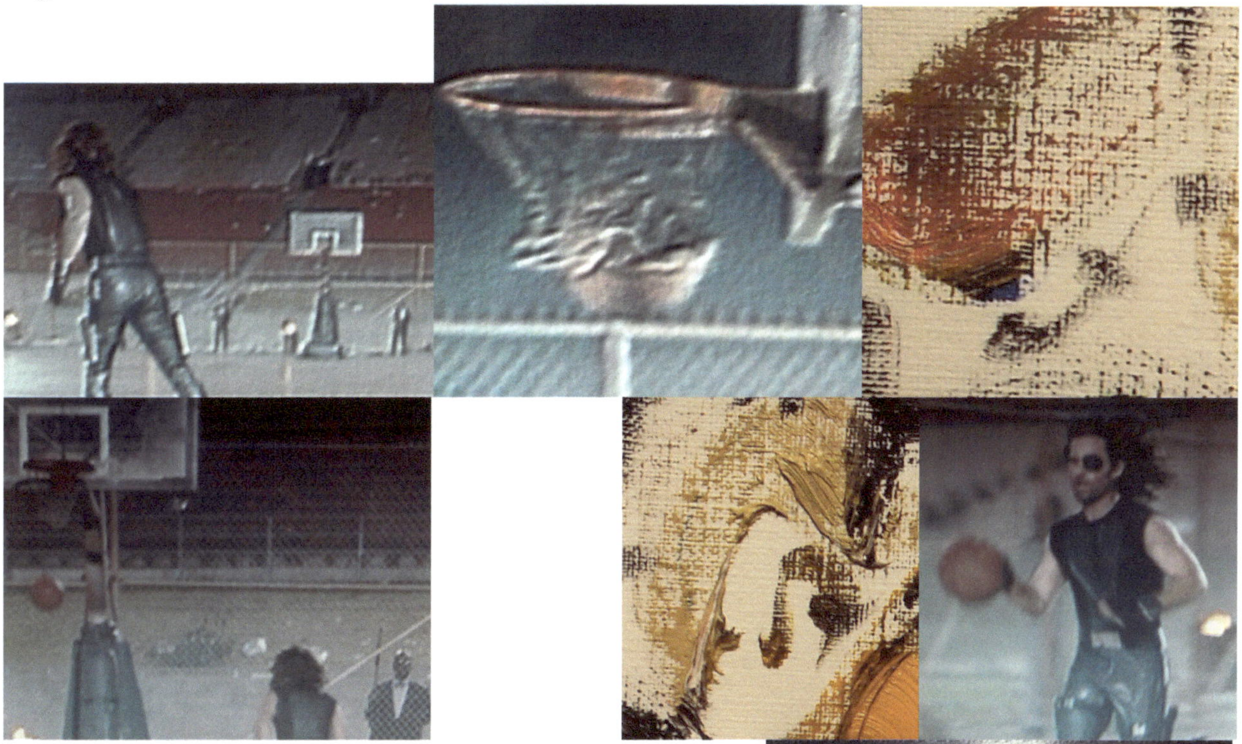

'Escape From LA' starring Kurt Russell - (above) the 'hog' large gun; basketball scenes and RV - Kurt Russell also starred in the original 'Stargate' movie .....

TIME LEAP

Security Alert Europe; France/Italy/Germany 2010; *find the three '4's in the Psi Paint below...*
(hint- RV often shows as reversed visuals, like a necker cube shift)

 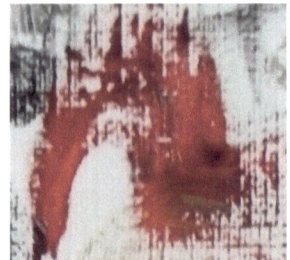 

Eiffel Tower & RV; visual time synch links to Eagle Nebula 6,500 ly (Hubble Heritage photo, STScI)

Deepside visuals; asteroids; Eiffel Tower, France match to structure lines, during Security Alert in EU

TIME LEAP

Psi Painting of the glorious CF-18 Hornet jets & trails shows - Edmonton, Alberta, Canada

Dairy Farm Wave of the Future at White Gold, Iraq 2010
- hearty & satisfying, rewarding occupations
Operation New Dawn

Richard Branson, Virgin Galactic 'Spaceship Two'; RV in gold tones, 3D

Space Ship Two - Mojave Desert, CA test flight Oct 11, 2010

Mars surface raw footage available online in the NASA/jpl raw data site. There is additional raw material on the surface that they do *not* have included up for public consumption. I was trained in Mars Reconnaissance during initial immersion weeks. They had a fax available I just ran my mouse pointer over the Cruise jewel box for a pop up fax. Spent ages working the surface of Mars footage when the NASA Rovers Spirit and Opportunity, the Mars Exploration Rovers or MERS were there just sending it back as Sol days photos. Fascinating hardly covers Mars Viewing and observational reconnaissance. Here are a few of the more publicly accessible photos of raw footage of the surface of Mars. Strange surface features along with some showing dots in the sky that are of 'other' than what is known. Any prints on the ground of horizontal line patterns are rover tread marks left as the MERs were tooling around taking the photos. They were designed to last for months. They worked for years. Just a few examples of odd: there was all manner of fascinating 'other' on Mars.

Mar's surface photos: Rover Spirit, Sol 768 & 753 dots in sky; Opportunity Sol 724 streak upper left

Strange white substance was splotched all over Mar's surface, showing in many raw footage photos; sometimes on the Rover's themselves, often just on the ground, also on areas surrounded by dark shadow. The photo next to it, shows some of the oddities found on Mars, they are too numerous to show here, and most of the photos I did as reconnaissance MRO, was by daily Fax from jpl and I did not keep any copy of given the highly sensitive nature of the material. Many strange and fascinating features and objects were revealed. These photos here are just from the raw footage of the SOL photos accessible online.

(above) Rover Opportunity Sol 645 & 649; more odd features on Mar's surface (below)

Satellite

Once you ride the dragon
And the Earth falls fast away
Leaving one's senses only
Future's past returned to stay.
A purple sphere of splendor
A tale of stars within.
Galactic forces transforming
As a gallant rides the spin.

A reflective curve crystallizes
Changing waves to silent flow
Spiraling deftly inward
As form begins to grow.
Multiplicity lending curls of colour
Fast and bright.
Sending messages of tranquility
Deep into the night.

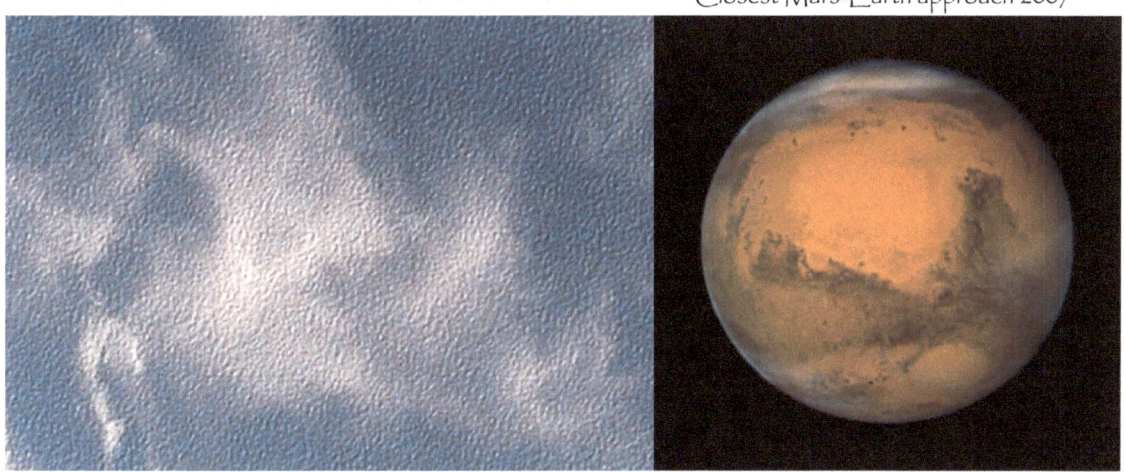

Closest Mars-Earth approach 2007

Now that would make a cool flag...for the Knights of Mars - MARS Land Claim
For anyone who needs to see a Flag to realize the reality of it all...the wisp was made by the
Canadian's Magic I think it's ecumenical dragon brooms. Maybe Puddingtons knows.

Silver was the casting
Of the seven stars that shine
While an indigo sky
Upturns the eye.
Brightens freely
Swift facets running infinite range
Over nature's design.

Blue Winged Pegasus
Orion's steed
Setting the pace
Plunging downwards through
Shifting galactic cores.

Starbursts coursing boldly
As distance
Echoes the vast chambers of space.

Winds of woven instinct,
Intersecting lines are thrown
Catching and uplifting light
As sweetly as pure tone.

Relying patterns yawn
As truths dance timelessly
Amid gossamer webs at dawn.

Across wind blown acres
Over sunlit skies
Sheafs of delight
Touch the laughter of eyes.
Rays of enchantment
A brazier of time.
Spells woven softly,
This heart tale of thine.

Drangons in hiding
Yet soaring in might.
Patient and soothing
Sound stroking sight

Troops Kandahar 2010; Sun Fire Ops - Canadian sky trails Edmonton, Alberta